HEALTH Need to Know

SilverTip

Stress and Emotional Health

by Ashley Kuehl

Consultant: Caitlin Krieck, Social Studies Teacher and Instructional Coach, The Lab School of Washington

BEARPORT PUBLISHING

Minneapolis, Minnesota

T0395129

Credits
Cover and title page, © Prostock-Studio/iStock; 3, © irin-k/Shutterstock; 5, © Taisiya Kozorez/Shutterstock; 7, © Olezzo/Shutterstock; 8–9, © ORION PRODUCTION/Shutterstock; 11, © cheapbooks/Shutterstock; 12, © Seahorse Vector/iStock; 13, © BAZA Production/Shutterstock; 15, © Jacob Wackerhausen/iStock; 17, © Sabphoto/Shutterstock; 19, © Olimpik/Shutterstock; 21, © Prostock-Studio/iStock; 23, © B-D-S Piotr Marcinski/Shutterstock; 24–25, © MDV Edwards/Shutterstock; 27, © monkeybusinessimages/iStock; 28, © mentalmind/Shutterstock.

Bearport Publishing Company Product Development Team
Publisher: Jen Jenson; Director of Product Development: Spencer Brinker; Editorial Director: Allison Juda; Editor: Cole Nelson; Editor: Tiana Tran; Production Editor: Naomi Reich; Art Director: Kim Jones; Designer: Kayla Eggert; Designer: Steve Scheluchin; Production Specialist: Owen Hamlin

Statement on Usage of Generative Artificial Intelligence
Bearport Publishing remains committed to publishing high-quality nonfiction books. Therefore, we restrict the use of generative AI to ensure accuracy of all text and visual components pertaining to a book's subject. See BearportPublishing.com for details.

Library of Congress Cataloging-in-Publication Data is available at www.loc.gov or upon request from the publisher.

ISBN: 979-8-89577-078-8 (hardcover)
ISBN: 979-8-89577-525-7 (paperback)
ISBN: 979-8-89577-195-2 (ebook)

Copyright © 2026 Bearport Publishing Company. All rights reserved. No part of this publication may be reproduced in whole or in part, stored in any retrieval system, or transmitted in any form or by any means, electronic, mechanical, photocopying, recording, or otherwise, without written permission from the publisher. Bearport Publishing is a division of FlutterBee Education Group.

For more information, write to Bearport Publishing, 3500 American Blvd W, Suite 150, Bloomington, MN 55431.

Contents

Under Pressure 4
Our Feelings, Ourselves 6
Ready for Action 10
False Fear 14
So Stressed Out 16
I've Got a Feeling 20
Feel, Think, React 22
It's All About You 26

Mind and Body 28
SilverTips for Success 29
Glossary 30
Read More 31
Learn More Online 31
Index 32
About the Author 32

Under Pressure

There is so much to do. After school, you have sports practice and homework. Plus, your parents want you to clean your room. And your phone is blowing up with messages from friends. All these pressures impact your emotional health. They can cause stress.

> A person's health has many parts. The mind and body work together to stay well. Emotional health is important. So is eating well, getting enough sleep, and exercising regularly.

Our Feelings, Ourselves

People often have many different emotions every day. Emotional health is how we handle these feelings. It involves **identifying** the emotions. It also includes how a person chooses to **respond** to them. An emotionally healthy person takes responsibility for how they **react** to their emotions.

> Emotional health is part of taking care of yourself. It's also important within strong relationships. Supporting friends and family is part of emotional health.

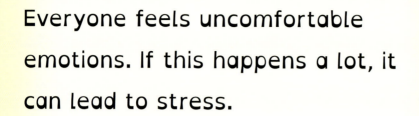

Everyone feels uncomfortable emotions. If this happens a lot, it can lead to stress.

Stress is a feeling of emotional pressure. It can be caused by many things. Starting a new school can be stressful. So can getting into an argument. When a loved one is sick, that can cause stress, too.

Stress often brings up many different emotions. A stressed person may feel angry, sad, or overwhelmed.

Ready for Action

Emotions start in the mind. But they impact the body, too. When a person feels anger or fear, the **nervous system** responds. This can happen with stress, too. The body reacts as if there is danger. It makes chemicals called **hormones**. This gets the body ready for action.

> When you feel stress, your heart rate may go up. You may breathe faster. Your body could start to sweat. Sometimes, people feel a tingle in their stomach.

Human bodies react to stress for safety. This gives them a burst of energy.

The stress response was very useful for ancient humans. It helped them get away from harm. If a hunter spotted a lion, they could use the extra energy to run away.

Some stress can be useful. The stress of a deadline may push someone to finish a big project. People may use the extra energy to perform well in a play.

False Fear

When there is no danger, the body is supposed to be calm. The nervous system helps it stay this way.

However, sometimes the body reacts to danger that isn't there. It can be hard to get the body to calm down when this happens.

> Speaking in front of your class cannot cause physical harm. However, your body may still respond as though you are in danger.

Public speaking is a common fear.

So Stressed Out

For some, stress is a common feeling. Others are rarely stressed. We all have different things that set off this feeling.

However, almost everybody has times when they face more stress. They may feel stress for longer than usual. This can lead to bigger issues.

> Feeling overwhelmed may be a sign that stress is growing. So is feeling angry more often than usual. Not enjoying things you normally like can be a sign of a problem, too.

Too much stress can lead to **anxiety**. This is feeling worried most of the time. Stress can also cause **depression**. People with depression go through long periods of feeling sad, angry, or not caring. Both anxiety and depression can make everyday tasks harder.

Anxiety and depression can be major challenges. People with these concerns often need help to get better. They may need to talk with a doctor. Sometimes, medicine can help.

I've Got a Feeling

People don't have much power over their body's reaction to emotions. However, they can learn to identify their feelings. They can also choose how to respond. This is called **emotional intelligence**.

Emotional intelligence helps people have control over their feelings. It can also be used to support others.

> Every person's brain is different. Emotional intelligence can be difficult for some people. They may have to work harder to understand and respond to feelings.

Practice can improve emotional intelligence, just as it can for other skills.

Feel, Think, React

There are many ways to **cope** with emotions. However, not all of them are healthy. One extreme emotional response would be to yell. This may feel good for a short time. But it is harmful to do often. Part of emotional health is figuring out healthy responses to feelings.

> An emotionally healthy person still has strong feelings. They just make good choices about what to do next. They react in ways that don't harm themselves or others.

Healthy ways to deal with emotions allow people to work through how they are feeling. Some people express their feelings through art. They draw, paint, or write. Others turn to physical activity. Moving their bodies makes them feel better. Mindfulness and meditation help many people, too.

A common way to handle stress is to talk with somebody. Friends, family, teachers, and coaches can all be good people to turn to. **Therapists** are trained doctors who help people talk about emotions.

It's All About You

Having a good handle on emotions is important. Everyone gets stressed sometimes. It can be hard to deal with. But with good emotional health, people can manage these feelings.

You only get one body and one brain. It's your responsibility to take care of them.

> Stress can put people at higher risk of other health issues. People may have stomach problems or headaches. Taking care of your emotional health prevents this.

Mind and Body

The body responds in many ways to strong emotions and feelings of stress. Here are a few things that can happen.

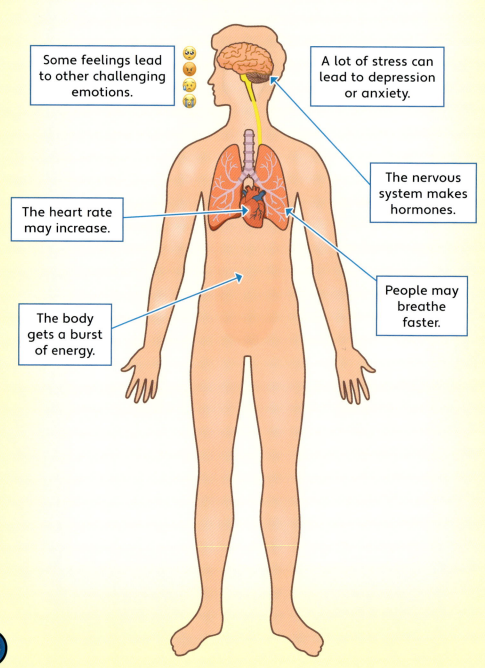

Some feelings lead to other challenging emotions.

A lot of stress can lead to depression or anxiety.

The heart rate may increase.

The nervous system makes hormones.

The body gets a burst of energy.

People may breathe faster.

SilverTips for SUCCESS

★ SilverTips for REVIEW

Review what you've learned. Use the text to help you.

Define key terms

cope
emotional health
emotional intelligence
nervous system
stress

Check for understanding

What is emotional health?

When a person feels strong emotions, what happens in their body?

Name an example of a healthy response to a strong emotion.

Think deeper

What could you work on to make your emotional health stronger?

★ SilverTips on TEST-TAKING

- **Make a study plan.** Ask your teacher what the test is going to cover. Then, set aside time to study a little bit every day.

- **Read all the questions carefully.** Be sure you know what is being asked.

- **Skip any questions** you don't know how to answer right away. Mark them and come back later if you have time.

Glossary

anxiety extreme nervousness or worry

cope to deal with and attempt to overcome a problem or difficulty

depression a state of feeling extremely sad for an extended period of time

emotional intelligence being able to identify, understand, and cope with feelings

hormones chemicals made by the body that trigger a reaction

identifying being able to tell what something or who someone is

nervous system the system that carries messages throughout the body

react to behave as a response to something

respond to say or do something in reaction to a situation

therapists people who are trained to help people with their mental health

Read More

Holmes, Kirsty. *Healthy Mind (Live Well!).* Minneapolis: Bearport Publishing, 2024.

Novak, Alex. *Stress (Coping).* Buffalo, NY: Rosen Publishing, 2024.

Roland, James. *Teen Guide to Managing Mental Health.* San Diego: ReferencePoint Press, 2024.

Learn More Online

1. Go to **FactSurfer.com** or scan the QR code below.

2. Enter "**Stress and Emotional Health**" into the search box.

3. Click on the cover of this book to see a list of websites.

Index

anxiety 18, 28

art 24

coping 22

danger 10, 14

depression 18, 28

emotional health 4, 6, 22, 26

emotional intelligence 20–21

hormones 10, 28

medicine 18

nervous system 10, 14, 28

react 6, 10, 12, 14, 20, 22

respond 6, 10, 12, 14, 20, 22, 28

therapists 24

About the Author

Ashley Kuehl is an editor and writer specializing in nonfiction for young people. She lives in Minneapolis, MN.